LABYRINTH HEART

NAIAD

THE POETICS
PUBLISHING

The Poetics Publishing is an imprint of The Poetics GmbH - a software and publishing company based in Zug, Switzerland.

For inquiries contact: naiad@thepoetics.eu

ISBN 978-3-03971-002-7 Paperback
ISBN 978-3-03971-003-4 Hardback
ISBN 978-3-03971-004-1 E-book

The Poetics GmbH
Hasenbüelweg 34
6300 Zug – Switzerland

For the ones who get lost within their
own hearts — I hope we can all walk each
other home, and if not then at least let
us be good company.

The things we reach for — Plants reach for the sun, people reach for the skies – always upwards and forwards. But lately I found my hands reaching for the earth. Reaching for where life comes from. Reaching for something to ground me. To remind myself that there's always time to return to the stars, to think of what is yet to come. But to remember what it is that carries me in this very moment. To not forget about my past. To see it as something that holds our roots but free to outgrow it in every direction and form. I reach for the earth to remind myself that everything that becomes has gone through mud. That life always begins in the dark, but it will end in sunlight.

Step into the labyrinth,
into the corridors of a heart
that doesn't even know
where it ends and where it begins.
Come in and see that you
are not the only one
who is wandering
in search of meaning,
of healing, of love.
And maybe it's not about finding
the way out of yourself,
maybe it's about going in deeper
and discovering what treasures
lie hidden within the centre
of all that you thought was lost.

Neither one of us was wrong,
we just weren't right for each other.
Sometimes good people
break each other's hearts.

You loved me
and I loved you
until one day we didn't.
Some stories are simple to tell
even if they were hard to live.

We are the lost ones — The ones that no brother comes to avenge. No sister to come and take care of us. No mother, no father to spend their whole lives looking for us. We are the ones who ended up where they had to because there was no other way. A tragedy, but not in the way that it is if we were one of those who could have been saved. No one to weep, no one to mourn for us, no funeral stands with their heads hung. We are the lost ones. The ones who belong where they are because we have no one else to belong to.

You never understood
my silence and that is why
you never understood
my words either.

I wish there was a way
to make you feel what I feel.
For you to feel the burn of your own fire,
to have your heart torn apart,
for you to feel what it's like
to have given it your all
and be left with nothing at all.
To feel what it's like
to love someone that only
loves himself.

I send my thoughts out on a search
for something new, but they always
come back with you.

How hearts shatter without touching the floor — Love can break your heart so many times without ever coming close to you. It's like air that kills you not when it's here but when it's gone. Like the knife that hurts but as long as it stays within you, you'll be okay somehow. It's not until you remove it, it's not until you have to feel the absence of it, that you bleed out.

And girls like me
were born with grief,
sadness belongs to us
just like our names.

And alone at night
I forget about all the times
you made me feel less-than,
instead I still remember
how it felt to be loved by you.
I forget the thorns
and only feel the petals.
I forget the teeth
and only feel your lips.
For a moment I forget
about the wolf in you,
for a moment
I remember you
as a boy who only
needed to be loved.

It was always easier
to love you in your absence
than it was when you were here.

NAIAD

A dare with the world — Life stands before me like a loaded gun. Being is a threat more than anything. It's like a dare. Dare to be happy, dare to fall in love, dare to be who you want to be – dare, and then watch how that will work out for you. Dare, and then watch how everything gets taken away. Dare, and see what happens when you fly too close to the sun. Dare, and see what the world will turn you into once you start believing you're worth loving, that you have the right to happiness. Dare, and find out how this place has never cared about any of your rights.

If life is one turn on the clock,
then we were the two hands
that only got to touch once.

They may say that
love never runs out
but I gave all
of mine to you
and now have none
left for myself.

She's a goddess of the in-between.
Stuck between leaving and staying,
loving and hating,
between regret and relief,
sanity and madness.
Wanting to open herself up but
craving safety.
Wanting to be held but
fearing to lose herself in its grip.
Stuck between wanting love but
fearing it just as much.

You were a comet passing through my life,
and I think how foolish of me to believe
that your love would burn for me forever.

Love is forever and then it ends — They tell me that it's better to have loved and lost than never loved at all, but every night I sit here and wonder if what we had was worth it. And I want to go back in time and tell myself that it's true that love like this exists, the kind you read about, the kind you wish for – it's real. But the part they never tell you about is that just because the love was real, doesn't mean it will last forever. Sometimes love is not enough, even if it should be.

My thoughts cannot
take a single step
without stepping on
something that you left.

I still look for you in every face I see.

If we're all just creatures of habit,
you seem to be the hardest one to break.
But I'm not sure I'm even trying.
I'm not sure I even want to.

Sadness and good daughters — Sadness wants to scream and rage and shout, but instead, like a good daughter, she hides in the dark. She hides in the silence. Sadness, like a good daughter on the surface, looks like someone calm, someone nice, someone who won't fight back. Sadness, like a good daughter, stays with you even if she wants to go. Sadness will always be yours, no matter how estranged you become. No matter how hard you try to shake it off. Sadness, like a good daughter, never leaves.

You cannot wish him into missing you,
you cannot pray him into loving you,
you cannot cry your way into his mind
or bleed your way into his heart.
He doesn't love you.
What else is there to say?
He doesn't love you,
no matter how much you do.

She looked at the cracks
in the pavement and thought
that maybe the cracks in her heart
weren't such a bad thing. After all,
that's where all the flowers grow.

This body still has muscle memory
and I worry that I'll never get rid of you,
that something in me will always
be reaching for you.

What I want for myself — I think I might have been obsessed with the idea of loving others, of showing them kindness, of forgiving them, of giving them a kind of saving. Thinking that in a way all of it would come back to me. Thinking that it would make them love me and forgive me. That it would make me love and forgive myself. Thinking that in the end, it would save me too.

I try my hardest to not see
love and you as the same thing.
I try my hardest to let go of you
and still keep love in my life.
I try my hardest to stop believing
in you, but still believe in love.
I try my hardest to be done
with you, but not with love.

This is your reminder — that no pain, no heartbreak, no grief will last forever. It feels eternal in the moment, but one day, and soon, all of this will seem so far away and so long ago. You will look around and realize that without you really noticing, the colours have started to become brighter again. I know you can't see it now, but life will make sense again. Love will find its way back to you and happiness is something that you will know. Something good has come to an end but let that give you hope that the bad things will as well.

And when I spill
"I'm sorrys" at every chance
maybe the forgiveness
I need the most
is not theirs
but my own.

People leave easier
than they come,
why then is letting go
so much harder
than holding on?

Getting over someone — can seem like an impossible thing. Especially since what we remember the most is often the best things. We keep replaying all the good memories, forgetting that there's always a reason why something had to come to an end. I think it's alright to grieve whatever we lost, no matter for how long it was ours (or even if maybe it was never ours at all), but it's also important to keep in mind what made us leave in the first place. We tend to romanticize things and people from our past, making it hard to see sometimes that the things we have now, and the things we can and will have someday, are so much better than any we left behind. The best is yet ahead of you, I promise.

When do I have to
stop hoping for us?
When do I have to
accept that you're not coming back,
that there won't be a text
from you waiting for me,
where you say you've got it wrong,
where you say I'm all you want?
When do I have to
let go of the illusion
that there's still a way for us?
When do I have to admit
that right person, wrong time
simply means
wrong person?

I am so far gone
from who I used to be,
some days I don't even
remember the girl I was.
But I still mourn her,
I still wish that I could
get her back.
Some days I start
to miss myself.

In your own orbit — Please never make your happiness dependent on someone else. People aren't always around, people inevitably hurt us, and people make mistakes. I know love can feel like the strongest form of addiction and that's why you have to learn to be capable of being without it. Because when you don't, you'll do anything to get the tiniest bit of it. You'll let people treat you however they want to if only they give you some attention and slivers of affection every once in a while. And you deserve so much better than that. So damn much better. Don't let them become so much of a part of you that you do not know where they end and where you begin. Where you cannot separate without losing all sense of who you are, without tearing yourself apart to get rid of the parts that belong to them. Let people add to your happiness and sometimes let yourself be sad over the actions or words of others – this is a normal part of a deep connection with someone. But never, please never, let them become the centre of your universe, the place you orbit around. Be your own star, your own sun. Cause god knows, you shine so bright.

I don't want the best thing about me
to be somebody else.

I'm just here hoping
that it's true what everyone says,
that there will come a day
where the pain has become
a distant memory,
where I'll be able to
look into someone's eyes
and not see yours.
I hope there will come a day
where I can smile at our good days
without the thought of
our bad ones breaking me.
The day where I can see
that losing you
was not the end.

Looking for a place to belong — Maybe the reason I haven't been drawn as much to the ocean as others have, is because I'm not looking for infinity or an endless horizon. What I need is to belong. For my eyes to be caught by mountains that don't block my view of the skies but bring me closer to them. I don't need openness, a seeming nothingness. I need paths with trees whose branches are reaching for me. I need for something to touch my skin, to tell me there's a place for everything to belong. I don't want freedom, I want a home.

~~I just wanted you to know…~~
~~The truth is that…~~
~~I need to tell you…~~

I think
I won't ever be able
to put into words
how much it is that you've hurt me,
how much that I miss you still,
how much it is that I loved you too.

I rise and I fall like the water in its cycle — Like the raindrop that knows it first has to fall, to bury itself deep into the ground as far as the earth will let it. That it first has to hit the bottom to be able to rise again. And rise I will. Softly, gently, unnoticed. With the fog, the mist, the haze. I won't make a sound, I will pass right through you. But rise I will. I will stand next to the storm brewing, next to the lightning. Drifting in a breeze preparing to rage, dancing with the hurricanes. I rise softly, but I come down like thunder.

Let burns be proof
that once there has been
warmth on my skin,
and what once was
will be again.
Let it be proof
that I will not
leave untouched,
that I have touched
others in return.

I'm not who I used to be — Changing is something completely normal and natural. Not only is it not a bad thing, but more so it's something that is actually necessary for your own growth. It's alright to want, like, and enjoy different things and to adjust accordingly. We learn and then we change. Bit by bit, in tiny steps like a sunrise until the darkness has turned into light and we didn't even notice when or how exactly it happened. Or other times suddenly, like a storm unloading, like an unexpected rainfall. And both of that is okay. Change your mindset, change your passions, change your looks (or don't), but whatever you do, don't apologize for moving forward, don't apologize for finding out what makes you happy.

It's strange but
sometimes it takes
distance to grow closer.
It takes letting go
to have it become
a part of you.
Sometimes it takes
leaving to realize
you want to stay.

She was never something — that simply reflected the world around her, something that took things into her hands and then put them back again. No, she became the things around her, she would absorb their energy, their light, their colour. When she touched things, they touched her back, grew into a part of her. She never had to reach up to touch the stars because they would come to her, they would reach for her. So when the light of the stars spilled across her skin, the light made a home of her too. It nestled into her hair like the night sky, into her eyes like the two moons of mars, all the way through her bones and into the depths of her soul like the universe – the starlight never left her.

I once believed
that a little love was better than none,
that a touch that burns is better than
not being touched at all.
I once believed
that second choice was better than
not being chosen at all,
that someone who hurt me was
still better than being lonely.
I once believed
that I have to take what I can get,
but not anymore.
I now believe
I deserve what
everyone else does too,
a love that heals,
a love that saves.

The multitudes within us — You can have thunder in you and storms in you, and still know peace, still bring peace to others. You can have a heart that's hardened and still touch people in the softest ways. You can feel the cold inside of you and still find warmth. Each one of us is so highly complex and complicated and difficult and full of contradictions, but that is the nature of all things. We all hold within ourselves the possibilities to be any kind of person – to be a different person at different times to different people. And sometimes people will see parts in you that you've never noticed or that you think you've lost or never had to begin with. And that's the beauty of all human connections – being seen for who we are, in all parts. And that through being recognized by others, we start to recognize ourselves.

What once was — It's easier to talk about pain that has passed. Pain that doesn't hurt anymore, that can't hurt anymore. It's easier to talk about struggles that I've overcome. To talk about feeling small when I'm standing tall. It's easier to talk about healing when I've done the work already. But I've never known how to talk about hurt that is present. About open wounds. Weaknesses that haven't turned into strengths yet. So when they ask me how I am, I say I'm doing fine, cause I cannot talk about pain still presently mine.

I knew that one day you'd
come back for me,
killers always return
to the scene of the crime.

A soldier misses the sounds of war — I think that often, especially when we're young (but anytime really), we go through relationships and friendships that are very raw and chaotic and wild. And we're all still learning what love even means in general but also what it means to us and learning what we want and need from it. So we find ourselves holding on to people that hurt us, people that we hurt in return, and we grow up thinking that's what love is supposed to look like. And when we find ourselves in healthy relationships, sometimes we feel like there might be something missing. Someone who has only ever known war, does not know how to live in peace until after a while, until they have learnt that they can stop surviving, stop fighting, stop questioning everything that comes their way. It is true that going through hard times together can make a bond stronger, but there's a difference between supporting each other in these times and between purposefully hurting one another, in setting fires just for the thrill of it. And I want you to remember that you don't have to go through trauma together (or even cause it to each other) just to prove your love.

You deserve a love
that's loud and clear,
do not settle
for question marks.

Sometimes it takes losing things — that you thought were an integral part of you – friends, a job, a relationship, the place you live in or a passion, for you to realize that none of these things made you who you are. Sometimes it takes failures, a forced change in direction for you to realize that the path you've been walking on was the wrong one all along. Sometimes it takes being proven wrong, being told about our faults to realize that something's not right, that we're not at peace with ourselves. Sometimes it takes seeing chances slipping out of our grasp so we can open up our eyes to new ones and be brave enough to take them. Sometimes it takes losing the one thing that you thought you wanted to realize what it is that you really need. Not every end is a loss, and not every loss is permanent. Be willing to embrace the change, sometimes that is all it takes.

Don't let someone who's confused
about their feelings and what they want,
let you become confused with what
you're worth and what you deserve.

I would have burned for you
but instead I've grown cold,
waiting for you to think it through.

I remember hearing people say — things like "you are the best thing about me" and believing it's such a wonderful thing to say, craving that kind of love, that kind of connection. Until I started thinking about it more and realized that while this is said out of love and admiration for another person it completely disregards the self. And it started turning into a sad phrase to me because I do not wish to turn away from myself, from my body that has given me so much, from my mind that keeps evolving and growing. The best part of me comes from within me and is a part of myself, not something that comes from outside, something that is added to me by someone else. Other people can make a better person out of us, they can bring out the best in us, but that's exactly what it is – they bring it out of us, from within, where it has already been as a part of us all this time. Other people can transform us, but they do not create. You are the only one that makes you you, and the best thing about yourself is always you.

Maybe we only get lost
so we can find each other.

It's not them, it's you — I think at some point we all realize that there's no way you can run from or escape yourself. That maybe the only constant in life is that you'll always have yourself, for better or for worse. And when we're unhappy we often blame it on things like our jobs, or not having a romantic relationship. And while all these things can be a part of it, the truth usually is that we're just unhappy with ourselves. That there are parts of us that we do not know how to accept, how to love, how to let other people see. And for as long as it is this way, no matter what's going on outside of ourselves, we'll never truly be happy. But if we do learn to accept and love ourselves, with all of our parts, then no matter what else is going on in our lives, we'll always be at peace with ourselves, we'll always have something to ground and shelter us from the troubles of the world. And I think that is the only way to be content. So if the only thing guaranteed in this life is that you'll always have yourself, then decide to make that a strength, a comfort. Be the friend, be the love, be the family you always wanted, you always needed. Decide to make a home out of yourself, a place to fall back into after a hard day because you will always be there to catch yourself.

She wears her past proudly
like the night sky,
every scar a star,
every bit of her
as perfectly chaotic
as the universe.

The people we choose — The people around you, the people you spend your time and energy on have such a huge impact on your life, and on you. So make sure to choose wisely and to choose with care. Choose people who love you unconditionally, who support you, who see the good in you and remind you of it. People who are full of passion and dreams and interests. People who are curious and open and empathetic but also people who will call you out, who will have the hard conversations with you – people who are honest with you about the good and the bad. Choose people who help you grow. Choose people who don't make you guess. Choose people who make time for you and you make time for them, but who will also remind you when it is time to choose yourself.

Where there's happiness,
there's gloom.
Sometimes we have to go
through winter, to appreciate
spring in its bloom.

The light in the dark — We all know that there cannot be light without there being shadows too, and that's what this is. If you have done bad things in the past, if you make mistakes, if sometimes you have terrible thoughts – do not be ashamed. We all go through this, it is a part of being deeply human. It matters not what things you have done in the past as long as you are willing to learn from them and are determined not to repeat them. It matters not to never make mistakes, it matters how you deal with them. It matters not to only think good thoughts, what matters is what thoughts you decide to act upon. There is light and darkness, bad and good in all of us and that is nothing to worry about. Even with darkness inside of us, we can be a light to others, and to ourselves. Without the darkness to stand against we wouldn't even be able to see the light at all, and what kind of world would that be – in which none of us has ever sat outside on the darkest and coldest nights to see the stars shine?

Make peace with your past
or you'll be at war with your future.

The view from rock bottom — There's something comforting about reaching the bottom. About knowing you have fallen and can fall no further. There comes a power with knowing that you've been through the worst and you survived. It's the kind of strength you don't ask for. The kind of wisdom not everyone will understand. Eyes that can see in the dark. Hands that know how to hold themselves. A heart that grows softer with every hurt because you've learnt the hard way that only soft things survive a fall and stay whole. Skin that is no stranger to sharpness, to cutting edges, to things that leave marks. Skin that has been loved. Skin that has been hurt. Skin that turned internal pain visible to the outside – the skin of a survivor. Skin that has lived and is every bit beautiful for it. And you can't change the things that happened to you, and you don't have to be grateful. But there's something to be said about going through hell and making it back. And if something exists in this world then it's a strange kind of balance – the lower your lows, the higher your highs. If you've fallen, you can fly.

They broke you bit by bit,
why do you expect yourself
to be put together all at once?

The sky never apologizes for its nuances — for the changing colours, for the grey, and for the rain. Because everyone knows that the sky cannot always be blue, that there must be day and there must be night. And I wonder why I expect myself to always shine, to never hide, to never let myself rest? Why I expect myself to be ever the same? Why grief or why sadness are seen as something bad, not something part of life like clouds passing by in front of the sun, here and then gone? But still always worthy of love no matter what it looks like, no matter how much it is able to give today. The sky never apologizes for its nuances, its hues and neither will I. So I'm changing like the sky, not always sunny but always worth the view.

She's golden at day,
silver by night,
even in the dark
she finds a way to shine.

The worst of times — bring out the best in us. I think every bad situation can also be a chance, a chance to re-evaluate, to get a new perspective, to realize what really matters and to fight for that – a chance to change. And with "best" I don't mean quiet, I don't mean obedient, I don't mean accepting things that you don't have to and shouldn't accept. What I do mean with "best" is that it is a chance to come together, to take care of and support each other, to lead with empathy but to also make yourself heard – say what you have to say, see the power that each one of us holds and which only multiplies when we stand together. What I mean with "best" is to fight for what is worth fighting for, even if it looks like a losing game.

I'm the wave and
I'm the shore,
both leaving and
being left,
saying goodbye but
wanting to stay.

Love sees you — at your highest highs and your lowest lows. It will see you at your best and at your worst, at your most vulnerable and at your strongest. It will see your breakdowns and it will see your triumphs. Love will see through every part of you and every part of life. It will challenge you and it will support you. And when it sees what you don't want to show, and yet it stays, and yet it grows, you will know that it is true. Because true love is never blind, it sees every part of you and accepts them all.

Saints of loneliness — I want to be a holly tree. Giving the last food of the winter to the birds when everything else has been frozen and covered with snow. I want to be a bench on an uphill climb. I want to be a tiny café on an otherwise empty train station late at night. I want to be a safe haven, a warm comfort to the lonely in this world. I want to hold your scars and say they're beautiful. And I want you not only to hear it but to believe it too.

When you love yourself
you'll always have a home,
no matter where you are.

Like the universe — she was both dark and full of light. A fixed star guiding you but still always appearing in different ways. Your favourite city that keeps growing but never loses its familiarity. A street that leads you home but not without surprises. Proudly showing her past while living her present and allowing you glimpses into the future. An awaiting adventure, a wonder left to discover, a mystery getting tangled in your hands. A heavenly body that longs to be seen, to be touched, to reveal itself to those who dare to try and understand. A silence so loud, a power so pure. Chaos and beauty, energy and peace, the force of a thing that knows how to keep its light even in the dark. So complex that she was hard to explain but so simple that deep down she could always be felt without needing to know how or why.

We tear ourselves apart
to be sun and moon,
to be sky and sea,
to be wild and tamed,
to be lover and saint,
to be woman and free.

I like to think of people as puzzles — Each complete on its own. All the parts already there. But sometimes, we need another person to come in and make sense of it all. Some won't have the patience and will give up. Some simply won't understand how all the pieces fit together. But there will be a person who will bring order to the chaos. Someone who will put all your parts together in the right way, who will see you for who you are. Someone who will love you whole and in pieces.

If you have loved once,
let that be proof that
you can love again.

Let us be like the mayfly
that is born with the rise of the sun
and dies before the light does too.
They do not know of darkness.
Like them, let us make
of our lives one day, not knowing
that before and after there is night.
Like them, for the little that we last,
let us know only sunshine.

You can't love people without needing them — I always felt like I had something to prove to everyone but most of all to myself, that I had to show how good I am at dealing with things on my own even if it wasn't necessary. Because I believed that's what true strength is – never needing anyone, always having the answers, and not feeling a damn thing while doing all of it. Not seeing that true bravery is letting yourself be seen, whole, the way you are. Not seeing that to build genuine connections you must let people in and let them help you. That being human means needing people and depending on them, that it means letting yourself be weak sometimes too. And I don't think that there's truly anything scarier but at the same time more beautiful, more like coming home than letting down your guard, your armour, and being seen and understood for who you are.

I don't know what to do
with all of this
longing inside of me,
where to put all this love that
keeps overflowing and spilling
with no one to give it to.

If you never try, you'll never know — There's only few things in life that you will immediately be good at. Most things take practice, take experience, take time to learn, to master – if ever. And it takes falling, stumbling, and failing until you succeed and even then, sometimes you will fall again. Few things in life are truly linear, most of it goes in circles and there's always more room to learn, to improve. But let that not be a sign of despair rather than a sign that there are always more things left to explore – more magic, more wonder, more hope, and more love. We might fall in hopes of flying someday but you can learn to find enjoyment in the fall too, enjoyment in the view from halfway down.

You reached into my heart
and planted seeds there.
You were gone before
you could see them bloom,
but I hope you know that
you've turned this wasteland
into a garden.
I hope you know that
you've made a difference
to someone somewhere.

It's easy to get caught up — in your own thoughts, in your regrets, your mistakes. In seeing the bad things you've done and the people you've hurt. You look at all that and you convince yourself that you're not deserving of anything good. But the truth is that we've all done things we're not proud of, and the fact that you know it was wrong shows how much you've grown. What has passed is past. It does not matter what has been, what matters is how you move forward from here on. What matters is that you decide to choose love and compassion, be it towards others, be it towards yourself. No matter your past, no matter the demons you have to fight, there is always a life worth living waiting for you. A life that isn't perfect but still a life filled with moments of affection, beauty, and joy – the kind of life you're deserving of, don't let anyone tell you otherwise. But especially don't let it be your own hands holding you back. If there's waves coming towards you, swim. If the air offers to carry you, let yourself fall. When life looks at you, hold its gaze and move towards it. And if a good thing is in front of you, be brave enough to take it.

She was a riddle
that didn't need
to be solved
to be loved.

Two of the same — A soulmate is someone who needs no explanation. Who knows exactly what you mean when you say it because their mind works in the same way as yours. Their heart feels in the same way as yours and you see colours with the same intensity. In another life, you might have been the same pair of lungs. A right hand and a left hand. A pair of eyes. Always aware of what the other tries to do, communicating without words. Two separate beings but still one. A soulmate is someone who understands you like only you understand yourself. Because knowing them is like knowing yourself.

Be brave, my dear
have a look at your fear.
What you thought was the end
were just clouds passing by,
what you thought was never-ending pain
was just a quick shower of rain.
Be brave, my dear
let go of your fear.
What you thought was your destiny
was just another changing season,
what you thought was a part of you
was just a passenger passing through.
Be brave, my dear
there's nothing left to fear.
The sky will soon be clear,
the light now so near.
Close your eyes,
feel the sun rise,
the warmth touching your skin,
see another life begin
where there's no fear.
And now you can rest
for you've been
so brave, my dear.

Remember when mother said — there's no such thing as bad weather, only unsuitable clothing? And maybe that's all life is. A series of sunny days and rainy days, of heatwaves and storms, tsunamis and droughts. And we cannot change the tides or control the clouds, all we can do is dress accordingly. Some days will require more protection than others. They will have you sheltering and hiding, covered in layers and layers. You will not let people see you, recognize you. On other days you'll be braver. You'll drop some layers. Let people come close to you, with no barrier, with no fright. What I'm saying is that there's a time for caution and there's a time for reckless bravery. But sunscreen is always a good idea. You never have to burn – not for the sun and not for love.

Self-love never shames you
for taking so long to embrace it.
It is only excited that you did.
It takes you by the hand and says:
"Welcome, we've got so much
lost time to make up for."

Dark matter — Most of the universe is made up of things we cannot see, things that stay in the dark. All we notice and all we perceive are the small parts made up of galaxies and planets and stars. So if you ever look at your own life and feel lost, like there's no place you belong, like there's no one who understands you, like you'll never feel happy again, remember that what you see is a very small part of the world and that there's so much more out there. Know that somewhere you'll find people who will take you for who you are, know that somewhere is a place you'll want to call home. And know that it is always worth to keep going even if only for all the things that are left to be discovered – all the cities and bookshops, all the songs and paintings, all the memories that are yet to be made. There is so much out there still waiting to be loved by you, there is so much out there still waiting to love you back.

My heart was a question
and your eyes had
all the answers.

I wish there was someone — who had been through it all with me. Who could see what it took to get to the place I'm in now. Who knows of the growth and the pain that comes along with it. Who understands what I've left behind and where I'm headed to despite who I've been, despite what everyone thought I would turn into. I want everyone to see what I'm capable of, how I went from whole to lacking and I'm still standing this tall. I long to be seen not for who I am but for the person that I've become.

He dressed
her in love
because that's
what she always
looked best in.

Summer melancholia — Summer can feel strangely melancholic at times, but there are days that you spend outside with friends, with a book, a drink, or strolling alone. Days where you feel the sunshine everywhere on your body, like it can just reach its rays inside of you and cover all there is, even the parts that have never seen the light, leaving nothing untouched. Days where life is just good because you realize you don't need much more than a sundress, good company, and a light breeze. Days where life is so simple, and so happiness is too. These days are fleeting like summer itself, you can't really hold them, like sunshine, you can only feel them. But when you do, it's good, so so good.

She was the energy set free when
stars die and planets collapse,
the power gathering in
the sky before a storm,
lightning about to strike.
She was the beauty and the
goodness in a world falling apart.

Passing it on — When time turns my body into a garden, I hope that something stays. I hope that when the daisies grow, they'll know about the prayers. And when a 12-year-old girl comes to pick them up on her way home from school and asks the question she thinks matters most, I'll tell her instead about all the people that do love her. And I'll tell her that life feels so grand right now but most of this won't matter when you've grown – except for the joy, the friendships, the time spent with your family. And when someone loves you in the future, you won't have to look for signs, only to them for they will tell you all on their own.

Falling in and out of love — You will fall out of love with me, many times. And it won't matter. We aren't perfect people, but we are as real as this love is. So I don't want you to live always being in love with me and with every single thing that I do or say. What I want is for you to live choosing me. Even when you are angry or sad or tired, that even so, at the end of the day you say: "You, I do not always know how or why, but it's you. A thousand times you."

You cannot change your roots,
but you can choose the places
you grow towards,
the things your hands reach for,
the people your heart beats for.
Even if your past was rough,
your future can still be a soft thing,
something that still has
so much more in front of it
than behind it.

I set it free, and it came back to me — The thing is, I do believe that every good you do will come back to you in some way. Maybe not directly. Maybe in a very unexpected way, but it does come back. The love and kindness you give to someone may not be returned by the same person, in the same day, or the same place. But everything is a reflection of us, of our actions, our intentions. The love you give will find a way back to you, in the moment you'll need it the most. Goodness is never wasted. You have to believe that.

She's a quiet woman
but the most powerful storms
never announced themselves
with thunder.

If my heart is like an ocean — you're the only one I let see it when the tide is low. I invite you in. Let you see through the depth, down to the ground. Everything lying bare before you, uncovered. I let you see what usually lies hidden beneath the water. I let you see the skeletons, the death, the bad things I've done, the things I regret, and the things I don't talk about — the worst of me. I let you see the corals, the amber, my treasures — the best of me. I even let you open the shells, my most guarded secrets, and I let you look at the pearls. I share them with you, I let you take them with you, let a part of me become a part of you. I let you see every fragment of me. And when the high tide comes, I pray that you'll stay. That you won't be afraid after what you've seen. I pray that you understand that I won't let you drown. That I will always carry you high. I pray that you're here for it all, for the highs and for the lows. I pray you're not afraid of the water.

Believe in yourself and you'll see,
the sky belongs to those
who dare to fly.

We all say that we want love — but oftentimes when there's a chance of it, we're afraid to take it. Loving someone from a distant, secretly, safely is one thing, but actually letting yourself be loved is a whole other thing. Love requires you to be vulnerable and for most of us there are few things scarier than that. You have to let yourself be seen wholly, you have to learn to share your thoughts, to voice your dreams, your fears, your frustrations. Even though you've been hurt and broken before, even though people didn't follow through on their promises – despite all of that you have to trust again. Love is the softest kind of bravery. So if someone wants to love you, please be brave enough to let them.

Quiet moments — I hope that you can find hope in the pauses, the interruptions, the breaks, the dead ends, the detours. I hope that you see that every empty space holds the possibility for an entirely new life. I hope you can find peace in the silence. I hope you can make your own way where there's no paved street yet ready to guide you.

She had learnt to survive
in unforgiving conditions,
for she knew that
no one can outrun a storm,
in order to survive one
you have to become one.
But she also learnt that
there's more to strength than destruction,
more to love than leaving ruins.
She was the eye of a storm,
at peace and tender,
sunny and calm.
While everything around her was
falling apart, she was
still standing in
all her gentle wildness, in
all her chaotic, unbroken beauty.

You came and you didn't try — to mend my cracks or to hide them. You came and you painted them golden. Turned them into something that draws the light, instead of hiding it. You came and you showed me that there's no shame in having a past, in failure, in pain. That all our dark parts can heal, that they can be turned into something beautiful if only we let the sunlight wash over them, if only we show them warmth. You came and you loved me whole.

We're not the same, and that's good — If there's one thing I learnt then that there's no other way to be happy except by being truly yourself, whether that's within an established and stable relationship or while freshly getting to know someone. There's a difference between taking an interest in something because you know the other person enjoys it, because you want to support them, because you know it will make them happy and between pretending you like the same things and need the same things just to seem easy-going and for the other person to like you. It's important to compromise, to get involved in each other's lives, but always stay true to yourself, have your own passions, and communicate what you need – because it might be different from what the other person needs. And remember it's totally okay to have different interests and opinions on certain topics. If anything, be open, stay curious, and learn from each other. Grow and change, but on your own terms, not for the sake of other people.

Everything's a sign,
if you're looking for it
and nothing will do,
if you don't want it to.

I hope
there's a love
that has seen it all,
and still decides to stay.

Long lost friends — I don't see sadness as my best friend anymore, and I don't miss it when it's gone. Now it's more like an old friend. Someone I have once spent many days with. Weeks and years where we would see each other almost every day. But by now I've stopped calling. Stopped asking for it to come over when I'm feeling lonely and all alone. But we still run into each other every once in a while, and I won't pretend I don't see it. I will greet it. Sit down with it. Hear what it has to tell me. Not daring to tell it that I've been doing better since we see each other less (even sadness has a heart and I don't intend to break it). Instead I enjoy its company that will always feel familiar. Thinking of the days when I was addicted to its poison. When we knew each other inside and out, when I was convinced it made me better – a better writer, a better listener, a better lover. And I don't think it ever had bad intentions, but sadness is supposed to be a traveller, a guest, a passenger, a fleeting season. And I never knew how to say goodbye to someone offering up a home. But today I know when it's time to leave and the parting comes easy. We pay our checks separately and go our ways. I've got other friends I want to meet.

Flames and embers — I don't think the goal is to become fireproof. To walk through fire over and over again, to stay in a place that burns you and learn to feel no pain. I think the goal is knowing when to run and when to stay. Knowing which fire will bring warmth and which one destruction. Listen, you don't have to let them burn you just to prove your strength.

To be honest,
the rain is still here,
but I'm starting to
let the sun in too.

Like the ocean — she was chaotic but gentle. Powerful enough to pull down the ships of those who only used her to get from one place to another. Strong enough to lift those up who had seen her depth and still weren't afraid of water, those who decided to stay, those who decided to dive even deeper. But soft enough to let herself be carried by the wind and the current to new adventures and new loves that were even greater than the ones before. So beautiful that everyone longed to be in her presence, to be reflected in her waves. For she had a way of making everyone shine. Like the ocean, she was chaotic but gentle, and beautiful, so dangerously beautiful. Both, capable of breaking and capable of healing.

And I'll be my own home,
like the earth,
planting flowers and trees,
nurturing my grounds,
letting things come to life
inside of me.

I'm a question, and you are the answer — So often things feel unclear and unsure, doubts arise. I'll ask myself whether I'm going down the right path, whether this is really what I want, and what I need. I sometimes ask myself if maybe there's something more out there. I feel good, but could I feel better? And my head has always been a gathering of "what ifs", but when I looked at you, I just knew. And I've never been so sure about anything in my life. Because most days I'm a question, and you are the answer.

Let your heart be soft,
what is soft does
not break.

What we're here for — We are not here to copy each other's beauty. We are not here to all become the same person, with the same faces, the same bodies, the same clothes we wear, and the same things we love. We are not here to hide from the sun and the rain from fear of what it will do to our skin and our hair. We are not here to starve ourselves of joy, individuality, or any food. We are here to dance wherever we are. We are here to look up at the sky and the stars and the far horizon over the mountains and over the sea. And most of all, we are here to love – others, the place we call home, the birds, the things that make our bodies happy and our minds, and ourselves – not in a few weeks or months or years, not only once we fixed whatever it is that we dislike about ourselves, not only once someone else shows us that we're worth it, not only when it is easy to do so, but right now. Make the most out of the days, for as long as the music plays.

It's okay if you want to go,
I won't stay here much longer either.
I'll just take a moment to say goodbye
to all the things we could have been
and all the things we were.
I guess I just thought we
would always stay here.

All the things you've been holding on to — The words you never said but wish you had, the dark thoughts no one knows about, the horrible things you've done but never told anyone, the things you secretly wish for but don't dare to say out loud – all these things you've been holding on to make your heart so heavy. No wonder some days life weighs on you like a burden you struggle to lift. You need to set yourself free. Say the words you've been so afraid of saying out loud. Let go of what could have been and what you wish would have gone differently. There's no changing the past. Put the weight down and let go. And you'll realize that breathing will not be as hard as it used to be.

Look at all that we've been through,
the heartbreaks, the love, the trials,
people have come and gone.
You and I, we've changed as well.
And maybe everything changed,
but a part of me still hopes
that something will stay.
That it might have been easier
to leave each other behind,
but that you still wander the walls
of my labyrinth heart
and can't find your way out.

NAIAD — Born to a multicultural family, Naiad has always been fascinated by the contradictions and multitudes inside all of us. Writing about the good, the bad, and all the in-betweens this world has to offer, she believes that the most important things are found in the small and ordinary moments of everyday life. Next to writing, she has a keen interest in film, literature, history, and contemplating life's little and big mysteries. Now she is thrilled to add her very first own book to her overflowing bookshelves, and is eternally grateful that you made space for it too.

Scan the code to discover more from Naiad:

More books from
THE POETICS PUBLISHING

What is Left of Us
Shreya Maurya

The Beginning is Near
Evenfall

Bullets and Silver Linings
Lorelei

Printed in Great Britain
by Amazon

31748670R00068